Haunted Inns of
Exmoor and North Devon

Robert Hesketh

Bossiney Books · Exeter

Acknowledgements

This book was made possible by the active co-operation of land-lords, landladies and inn staff who generously shared their supernatural experiences with me and were so helpful in showing me their haunted inns and in facilitating the photographs. Thanks also to my wife, Adrienne, who accompanied me on my investigations and ably assisted with interviewing and with her own insights into the unseen worlds around us.

The photograph on the front cover shows the bar at the George and Dragon, Ilfracombe (page 16). The title page shows a historic photograph of the Plough Inn at Holford (page 25).

First published 2022 by
Bossiney Books Ltd, 68 Thorndale Courts, Whitycombe Way,
Exeter, EX4 2NY
www.bossineybooks.com
© 2022 Robert Hesketh All rights reserved
ISBN 978-1-906474-97-3

All photographs are by the author, www.roberthesketh.co.uk
Historic photographs are reproduced with the permission of their owners.

Printed in Great Britain by Booths Print, Penryn, Cornwall

Beggar's Roost, Barbrook near Lynton

Dating from 1683, the Beggar's Roost is an amalgam of the former Exmoor Manor House (the hotel area) with what was a shippon and is now the pub. There we talked to former London police officer Kevin Denney, who's been landlord of the Beggar's Roost since 2015.

'I'm very sceptical, but keep an open mind,' said Kevin. 'By this, I mean I don't believe 99% of the stories I've heard, especially as many of them are drink-induced. For instance, there's a cold place in the pub area, between the glass-fronted door in the outside wall and the door to the toilets, where six people have independently told me there might be a supernatural presence. However, there's no heating there, the heating comes from the wood-burning stove by the bar, so – as a sceptic – I can explain that away.

'All the same, I can tell you with certainty about a couple of incidents I've witnessed first-hand which I just can't explain away. I'm always the last person to leave the bar at night and the first person down in the morning. No one can get in here between-times except

3

me. Now, behind the bar there are pint glasses on a shelf at waist level and placed the wrong way up. I came down one morning and found three of them on the floor, the right way up and equally distanced from each other. I have no idea how that happened.

'More recently, my wife and I were in our apartment above the hotel where we saw something neither of us could explain. We have a bin there with a spring-loaded lid. When you press the lid down it shuts; press it again, the catch is released and it opens, pushed up by the spring. Well, we were two feet apart talking to each other and watched as the lid closed on its own and then opened on its own.

'When I was in the Police I heard lots of tall stories and when I'm at the bar I'll hear ten versions of the same story from locals. In their own minds, their story is factual, but there are things that are mistaken or exaggerated or whatever… told for entertainment or embellished every time it gets told.

'We had a Psychic Supper in the Function Room upstairs, attended by six psychics, among them a mother and daughter. I don't know whether it was a put-up job within the family, but as they came into the bar the daughter said, "Have you seen her?" To which the mother replied, "Yes, I've seen her."

'They swore there was an old lady in the far corner of the bar. I looked, but I couldn't see anything – of course – but I didn't ask for a description of the old lady as they would have seen I doubted their word. Anyway, they gave us a good night's entertainment if nothing else. I was busy down here, serving in the bar, but everyone who attended enjoyed it. Some took it very seriously, some not so.

'Here am I saying I'm a sceptic, but every night I pass that corner and I say "Goodnight, Mary," because if there is anyone, we call her Scary Mary – just because it rhymes. I'd love her to speak to me or whatever she is to show herself to me and then I could have a bit more of an understanding.

'There is another story I can recount. It's not first hand, but credible I would say, from personal experience. Three years ago a gentleman who'd stayed the night in Room Four came into the bar. He said he didn't believe in ghosts or spirits or anything like that, but he was never going to stay in that room again.

'Naturally, I asked him why. He replied there was someone in the wall trying to get out, adding "I know this sounds ridiculous now, but I was stone cold sober and that's what happened."

'His wife was taking the mickey out of him, as was I a little bit. We convinced him he should go along to the room, but he said, "No, it's different now," as he showed me the wall. In that he was poo-pooing his own story it seemed to have some credibility.'

Were there, we wondered, other guests who had had strange experiences at the Beggar's Roost?

'When the previous landlord was here, two guests claimed they saw a woman walking across what is now the breakfast room, a mezzanine area, above the function room,' said Kevin. 'In my time, another guest claimed he felt a hand pressing against his chest all night long. When his wife looked at him, she saw a red hand print, not his own, on his chest.

'Despite what I've told you, I feel perfectly at my ease here. If there was any malice from anything it would have happened by now as we've been here six years.'

Coaching Inn, South Molton

South Molton's Coaching Inn in Queen Street is said to be over 300 years old and stands by the old post-road which led from Barnstaple to Dulverton and on across the southern edge of Exmoor to Bridgwater. Countless local customers and travellers have crossed the threshold: some continue to make their presence felt.

'I have never felt threatened, nor sensed that any spirits here were going to harm us,' said landlady Jayne Morton. 'I have always said thank you to them for sharing their space with us and refused to have any sort of séance or cleansing rituals, reassuring them that this is their home and sanctuary too.

'All the same, locking up late at night was always a little nerve-wracking when alone as the place is huge. There used to be a long red curtain across the function room doors that always moved. Although it wasn't ominous, it just felt a little nervy as if someone was watching you. Suffice to say, none of the staff liked to lock up.

'One night there was definitely a presence there, a shadowy shape looking like a large, long-haired man. It wasn't until some time later that a medium detected a long-haired man in the function room, looking, he said, like a warrior type, bare chested and with multiple necklaces on. I was told this was possibly my guardian as I was going through a bit of a rough patch.

'My late dad used to smoke cherry pipe tobacco and there have been multiple times people or staff have told me they can smell it. I truly believe that my dad would have been a huge asset to the pub and visits me regularly. When my grandson was born I left him asleep in the carvery area and he woke up screaming. I thought nothing of it, but then was told by a medium that she had a message from my dad, that he was sorry for scaring the baby, he just wanted to see him and to check that no other spirit was worrying us here.'

Several people have sensed the presence of a small girl at the Coaching Inn. 'A young girl used to sit in a chair by the bar,' said Jayne's sister, Jill Jones. 'We call her Betty. A customer once went to sit in Betty's usual chair, but jumped up saying she couldn't sit there as someone had already taken it.'

'I see her in my mind's eye,' said Adrienne. 'She's about seven years old, but she's small for her age and looks younger. She's wearing a frayed white dress and a poke bonnet, possibly made of straw. Her costume is difficult to date; it could be Victorian or early 20th century. A fun child, she has dark eyes and a tanned complexion. If you try to ask her about herself, she's very reticent.'

Betty is very mischievous according to Natasha Halls, who has worked for several years at the Coaching Inn. 'She moves things around, smashes glasses and messes with the gas taps in the cellar, which you need a spanner to move. I think it was she who pinched my bottom.'

Natasha lives on the first floor of the inn: 'We get a lot of footsteps along the corridor, banging on the walls and creaking. My door used to rattle around two a.m., so I lock it now. When I was redecorating my bedroom it was full of hovering blue orbs.'

Jill too has had some strange experiences while staying in the room now occupied by Natasha. Once she was woken by some presence pulling the blankets off her bed. At other times, the TV, kettle and lights would turn themselves on and off.

The Exeter Inn, Chittlehamholt

Chittlehamholt's Exeter Inn is a Grade II listed building of the late 16th or early 17th century. Typically Devonian, it is built of stone and cob with a thatched roof and was a farmhouse before it became a pub. It has seen a great many visitors over the generations, serving travellers on the old route between Barnstaple and Exeter, as shown in John Ogilby's road atlas *Britannia* of 1675.

The past is very present at the Exeter Inn, as Adrienne and I found when owners Steve and Hazel Bowles introduced us to two of their regular customers, Helen Hollick and her daughter, Kathy Blee. Helen and Kathy live in another of the village's twenty-four listed buildings and are convinced that both it and the Exeter Inn are haunted.

Six of us and the Bowles's lively dog, Frankie, made ourselves comfortable by the pub's cavernous fireplace and talked through the dwindling light of a winter's afternoon and into the evening.

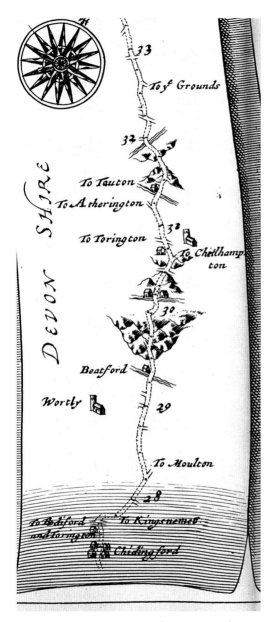

Part of John Ogilby's route map dating from 1675, in which Chittlehamholt is referred to (erroneously) as 'Chidingford'

A strong rapport grew between Adrienne and Kathy, as they developed a shared sense of scenes from the inn's history, describing them in vivid detail.

The first scene Kathy and Adrienne described involved a group of men in Victorian costume discussing business: land and boundaries. There were two main actors. One was a tall, dark-haired man with a neatly trimmed beard. Smartly dressed with a pinned cravat, he carried a riding whip and was standing. The second was seated. Less smartly dressed, he was smoking a pipe (Kathy could smell the tobacco) and used his pipe to emphasise his points as the discussion grew more heated.

Behind this scene, the two women sensed another, much earlier, scene, this time from the English Civil War. Again, what they envisioned was a group of men. Royalists, possibly a troop, maybe an *ad hoc* group of stragglers, they appeared to have been involved in fighting, possibly at the Battle of Torrington, which was fought on 16 February 1646, some dozen miles to the west of Chittlehamholt. It concluded in a Parliamentarian victory, with a further bitter blow for the King's supporters when Royalist prisoners held in Great Torrington church with the captured guns and powder were killed in a massive explosion which destroyed the building. This and the Royalists' earlier defeat at Bovey Heath on 9 January effectively ended Royalist resistance in the West.

As Kathy and Adrienne described it, the men have come to the inn knowing the landlord's sympathies are with their side – though he would be wise enough to be equally accommodating to their enemies. They are talking animatedly about the fighting and what they should do next.

One is wearing a red coat, breeches and riding boots. Kathy believes he is called Richard. At his side Richard has a cavalryman's sword, suggesting he is an officer. Blond and bearded, he is mud-spattered and his clothes are torn. The middle finger of his right hand has been injured. He stands proudly, trying to disguise his overwrought nerves and the further pain and discomfort he suffers from an old wound to his left hip which was caused by a musket ball that was later removed. He is drinking beer which has been given him. This smells strongly of hops and there is also an odour of rosemary and lavender strewn on the floor. He has asked the landlady to keep a careful watch from an upstairs window.

Another man is leaning against a wall. He is also muddied and his clothing is torn and tattered, as though he has had several tumbles in effecting his escape. He too is on edge and is urging his fellows to keep on the move. Adrienne had a strong impression of their anxiety and felt they have plans to evade pursuing enemy troops by heading south across Dartmoor to take ship from a port in south Devon to safety in France. With the evening coming on there is no time to lose. Their anxiety is further heightened by their lack of local knowledge as they come from another part of England, Bristol or Gloucestershire. Thus they would need a guide. However, they have horses and Richard is showing the gold coins he has, but asks what use the money is unless they can escape.

A third man is seated with a tankard. He is strongly built and swarthy. Like his fellows, he is begrimed. His dark blue clothing is torn and he has lost a tooth. He is smoking a long clay pipe with a small bowl. The fourth man has auburn hair. He is slender and dressed in dark green. He relieves his unease by pacing up and down, spilling some of the beer from his tankard as he does so. Pale and withdrawn, he too has been hurt.

The group are in a bind because their horses are exhausted and it is late in the day. They face the prospect of riding into the night and having to seek shelter from strangers who may betray them.

Kathy next saw a farm boy of about ten years old appear to tell them that two fresh horses have been found. He is going to take Richard's lamed mare away to a safe place where Parliamentarian troopers will not find her and draw their own conclusions from the brand on her side. The mare has a flesh wound which will heal. She is a fine horse and no bad exchange for the two horses the boy has brought. At this point, there was a pause in our talk until landlord Steve asked: 'What intrigues me is why you see these people, as they were only here briefly at the inn and moved on?'

Kathy pondered the question, before replying: 'It's because it was an important, emotionally charged occasion. There was a lot of energy about.'

'In a different way, the Victorian scene was important to the actors involved too,' Adrienne added. 'They were haggling over land, ownership and boundaries.'

The former forge

We moved on to the dining area behind the hall fireplace, where Adrienne and Kathy could smell burnt wood, although I could not. This area is now roofed, but Kathy and Adrienne had the impression that it was once open to the sky, a forge and a place with a lot of hustle and bustle where people and horses congregated.

Kathy's vision was of a strongly built young blacksmith, dressed in 18th century costume: 'He's a quiet chap, not overly interested in people, more at ease with horses. He just wants to get on with his work and finds the group of over-talkative women hanging around his forge a nuisance.

'I see a very gossipy blonde. She's trying to look elegant, but she isn't. She's what you might call "mutton dressed as lamb". The centre of attention, she dominates the giggling girls around her. I feel she has a crush on the blacksmith, but he's not interested in her or the girls, who he thinks are stupid. He's interested in someone else, a quiet, plainly dressed girl carrying a basket of rushes.'

'She's wearing a brown dress and a white chemise,' added Adrienne, 'but this doesn't disguise her prettiness. She has light brown hair and a slightly rounded face, with rosy cheeks and hazel eyes.

'Ah, the giggly girls have pushed off. They're calling the shy girl to follow them, but she's gone over to talk to the young smith, or rather to the horse he's going to shoe, crafty thing. She's worked out the way to approach him is to talk about the horse. He's going to have to put his foot down if he wants to marry her, because there's someone else who's interested in her. Also, she's non-conformist, which will make things difficult for him, but he's made up his mind that she's the girl he really wants.

'I feel we've picked up this moment because it is such an important moment in their lives, a deciding point. He's determined to go to her parents and ask for her hand in marriage. He's not quite the person they would have chosen – a non-conformist minister would have been ideal – but they're impressed by his ardour and seriousness. They'll speak to their daughter and she'll agree.'

We returned to our seats and Steve brought another round of coffee. The talk resumed, but Adrienne had the impression an elderly man was at the bar listening in.

'He's grey haired and broad shouldered, smoking a cigarette,' said Adrienne. 'His hair is flattened down as though he's been wearing a hat. I feel he belongs to the early part of the last century. He's grumpy and unfriendly, nobody likes him.'

'I think he was the landlord,' interjected Kathy. 'He might be the man called Bill Boucher in the photograph in the bar. He's sitting on an Exmoor pony. Neither of them looks happy!'

Before we left, we stopped in what had been the snug in times past when men and women tended to socialise separately. Whilst the public bar was largely a male preserve, women favoured the snug, which consequently had an atmosphere of its own.

'I can see a group of older women from the 1950s,' said Adrienne. 'All of them are wearing hats. Frankly, they're a bunch of old gossips and they're talking about a young man in the village, saying "He'll never make much of himself," and cackling about it.'

'They're trying to be elegant, drinking cherry wine from small

The Exeter Inn, Chittlehamholt

A historic photograph of the Fox and Goose at Parracombe

glasses,' added Kathy. 'One of them is a younger, recently married woman, a tradesman's wife. She sticks out like a sore thumb, not only because she's young, but because she's wearing brighter, more modern clothes, a pastel pink dress. She's been dragged in to this party and is trying awkwardly to make her excuses and leave the room. My impression is she and her husband would later move from the village and this gathering was a deciding point in her future.'

Fox and Goose, Parracombe

Parracombe's Fox and Goose began as a couple of thatched cottages and later became a coaching stop on the Ilfracombe to Lynton route. Photographs in the bar show the inn with coach and horses outside. These depict it both before and after its expansion and alteration in 1894 by Henry Blackmore, a relative of R D Blackmore, the author of *Lorna Doone* (1869), a dramatic romance set on Exmoor.

Henry Blackmore continued as landlord until 1922, despite a severe setback when he was kicked in the leg by a horse so badly the limb had to be amputated. Possibly it is Blackmore's spirit that haunts the inn, or maybe that of the unhappy man who is said to have drowned himself in Pinkery Pond on Exmoor after his love for a barmaid at the Fox and Goose went unrequited.

Nikki Houle, who has been landlady since 2004, is non-committal, though she is inclined to believe the presence she has sensed here is male: 'Before we came here, I imagined I'd be bothered by the supernatural, but I wasn't, it's been quite comforting. There's no negative energy here at all.

'Both my husband, Paul, and I have often seen things out of the corners of our eyes, but when we look up... there's nothing there. Things were apparently stirred up by the recent renovations. Paul was walking up the stairs one day when he saw a shadow, which he followed up, thinking someone was ahead of him. Reaching our flat, he called out, but nobody was there.

'A guest asked if we had spirits here. I'm always non-committal if asked this question and said, "Maybe, I wouldn't like to say for sure." He said, "I've definitely felt something upstairs in Room 3."

The Fox and Goose

'Another of our regular customers is very open to seeing things. He's a specialist in reiki – they're into universal energy and hands-on healing. Well, when he stayed here he remarked – again without any suggestion from us – that there is something active in Room 3 and that there's a little girl who comes to the table.

'After we finished the refurbishment, particularly after we'd finished work on Room 3, things went very quiet. The inn has a different feel now. I actually quite miss the way it used to be, which is weird. It had given me a happy feeling… whatever had been there has been released.'

George and Dragon, Ilfracombe

The George and Dragon is Ilfracombe's oldest inn and a listed building. Behind its massive stone walls are exposed ceiling beams and two large stone hearths with wooden lintels, both carved with the year 1641 – though the inn is thought to be far older than that, with the year 1360 found inscribed on a door.

'We took over the George and Dragon in 2004 from my sister, Chris,' said landlord Jon Quinn. 'I'd never had any supernatural experiences before we stayed here as Chris's guests and our radio mysteriously switched itself off with a click. "That'll be Celia" said Chris when I told her.

'We have an apparition, an old lady, who sits in a quiet corner of the bar. I've not seen her and I don't want to see her, but other people have, a dozen times or more. She sometimes appears behind customers, mainly through the summer. People make way for her – and then realise she's disappeared.

'In the bar is a fabulous photograph of an old lady in period costume sewing and several customers have said "That's her with a
different hat, a white one, not the dark one in the photo." She's the
one we call Celia. 'It was fascinating to have mediums here. One
told me we have fifty or sixty spirits in the pub. Not all of them are
associated with the George and Dragon; some may have come with
the recycled ships' timbers and ballast that have been used in various repairs. I was relieved when the medium told me they're quite
happy and settled. I said that's the way I'd like it to stay – though
occasionally they're a bit mischievous, tapping you on the shoulder,

moving things around and turning lights on during the night for instance.

'Ladies have also been locked in the toilet cubicles. Some get quite hysterical. I think it's the wet weather swelling the wooden doors and jamming them, but twice when I've told the spirits to stop messing about we've been able to open the doors directly, which is something I can't explain.

'The house across the street was once a brothel. One of the ladies had a son by a farmer from Watermouth, a regular customer. This boy is said to be around the back of our pub by the cellar, posted as a lookout for smugglers, who were very active all along the North Devon coast, not least in Ilfracombe, where a Revenue cutter was stationed.

'We have a cellar, which seems to have had tunnels – now bricked up – linking it to a path at the back of the pub called Rupert's Wood. This leads discreetly through the town and down to the cove side of the harbour.

'A local paranormal group did some fantastic investigations here, setting up their equipment after we closed at eleven and staying till three in the morning. It was they who claimed to make contact with the lookout boy, but not surprisingly he was not willing to talk much.

'We've had several other paranormal people here. One group, also very well equipped with detection devices, was particularly looking for electronic pulses. All of a sudden I saw these orbs of light, which they said might be animals; then some larger orbs appeared. I said, "Now, you know me, I live here. Please show yourselves." One orb appeared on my left and one on my right. This happened five or six times more. It was absolutely intriguing.

'Another medium talked to a spirit in the bar who said she was the mother of eleven children who all died in a fire here. The medium knew I had no previous knowledge of the fire, but told me I'd see evidence of it at some point. I didn't like the way she predicted things, but lo and behold a few weeks later we had a lot of rain and some of the masonry came away and behind it we found charred wooden beams.

'I'm sceptical in some ways, but I've been at the George and Dragon so long that I just live with what's here. I talk to the presences, telling them I don't want to see them – but they've not talked back to me. We've had a lovely time here and we've never felt uncomfortable with anything we've found unusual.'

Golden Lion, Barnstaple

'We think we're the oldest working pub in Barnstaple,' said landlord Mick Simmons as we explored the Golden Lion. A Grade II listed building in the Square, it dates back at least to the early 17th century and has a many-layered history, having been altered and added to several times, particularly in the early/mid 18th century, when it gained its impressive facade.

'I'm a sceptic, but I've seen things here which I just can't explain,' Mick continued. 'We have three ghosts. One is a small girl. She occupies the stairs. Sometimes she taps me on the back or pulls my shirt. A common occurrence is for glasses and the odd bottle to jump off the shelves behind the bar. Another time a picture fell down for no reason.

Courtyard at the Golden Lion

'There's nothing threatening about her, she's just a child, but a bit mischievous. If I tell her to stop her tricks, she does so right away. The story is that she met her death when she fell down the stairs and into the cellar below – though this has been filled in since then. I believe I saw her once as a white mist which passed right by me. It was about three in morning, but I was stone cold sober, so this wasn't alcohol induced.'

'I've seen orbs of light floating across the screen on the CCTV in the pool room,' added landlady Tracey Benson. 'It happened again when I was watching images from the downstairs passage on the office CCTV, but that time the orbs were moving in jagged diagonal lines. It was most bizarre. They were definitely not caused by specks of dust or a flying insect, but by orbs of light.

'A woman, a medium, who visited the pub confirmed we have three ghosts,' continued Tracey. 'There's the little girl Mick told you of and a woman who wanders around upstairs in the cocktail bar. There's nothing frightening about her, but I associate her with the beam-activated light up there which turns itself on and off for no reason at all.

'The medium also spoke of a nasty old man who murdered somebody in the cottages which were once at the back of the pub

and who now haunts the back stairs. The first time I used those stairs I had the disconcerting feeling that someone wanted to throw me down them. It was weird... I'm not over-sensitive, but I didn't use those stairs for ages.'

'Even I've had feelings that I'm not welcome in that part of the building,' added Mick. 'It's a proper unpleasant feeling too and even in the height of summer it's always cold there. Nonetheless, I'm not going to be bullied out of using that area.'

Mick continued our tour of the inn. We crossed the main court-yard, which is overlooked by a timber-framed gallery and links the two major parts of the building. Passing through the old carriage way, we mounted the main stairs, where apparitions have also been reported by a member of staff, and arrived at the cocktail bar.

'Sometimes you have the feeling of being watched,' said Mick, 'especially here, upstairs. A couple of people have told me they've been watched at the cocktail bar and from the courtyard below. Jimmy, who worked here, said he looked up from the bar and saw a face looking back at him. The apparition then waved at him... at which point he left in a hurry!'

Heanton Court, Heanton Punchardon

Now an inn and restaurant, Heanton Court occupies an imposing situation overlooking the Taw estuary between Barnstaple and Braunton. The seat of the powerful Basset family from the 15th century to 1802, it is a Grade II listed building and much older than it at first appears. Its battlements, well-proportioned windows and heavy keystones apparently date from remodelling in the 18th century. It was further altered in the 19th century, when part of the building was lost to the railway. There were more alterations in the 20th century and further recent refurbishment.

However, its most poignant supernatural manifestation dates to the English Civil War. Devon was bitterly divided between King and Parliament, with the Bassets and Heanton Court favouring the Royalist cause, though support for Parliament was strong in much of North Devon, including Barnstaple.

We are indebted to local author and medium, Sue Pengelly and to Alan, who lived at Heanton Court as a boy, for the following account:

'Alan told me he'd had various experiences at Heanton Court,' said Sue. 'However, his Dad didn't believe in ghosts at all and was scathing about it.

'When the family had some friends come and stay, one of them and a dog shared the same bedroom with him and his sister. During the night, the older girl, then aged around thirteen, awoke to hear the dog growling and to see a girl in a blue dress walk between the beds and disappear straight through the wall.

'The story he later found concerned a farmer's daughter, who was in love with a man involved in the Civil War. Looking down from Heanton Court, she could see him on the landing stage on the bank of the estuary, but she could also see – which he could not – a hostile party of Roundhead soldiers approaching down the lane. In her desperation to get his attention and save him from them she fell from the third storey window and died on the grass below. She was wearing a blue dress.

'Alan went on to relate two encounters his father had with the girl. In the first, he was approaching home when he noticed a girl in a blue dress looking out of an upstairs window. Thinking it was his daughter, Lizzie, he waved to her and she waved back, but when he entered his kitchen he found Lizzie sitting at the table – but she was not wearing a blue dress.

'Another time, Alan's family were all sitting and talking over lunch on Christmas Day, when his father suddenly stopped talking and saw the ghost of the girl in blue himself. After that, he couldn't say that he didn't believe.'

Sue told me she herself had visited the bedrooms upstairs at Heanton Court, but had not found them particularly spiritually active. However, staff had had supernatural experiences before the building's recent refurbishment and change of ownership. These experiences were nothing frightening, just the sense that someone who once loved the building had been back to visit, obviously the girl in the blue dress looking for her man.

Plough Inn, Holford

Parts of the Plough Inn at Holford on the eastern flank of the Quantock ridge are thought to date from the 16th century, although it has been altered and added to since, as landlady Michala Crossley and Head Chef Richard Brunt explained when we talked by the fireplace in the lounge, the oldest part of the building.

'My bedroom's directly above us,' said Richard. 'When Chris, the old landlord, was here it belonged to his daughter. One day he heard the most almighty screams. He ran out to find her in distress, claiming someone had got into bed with her. When he went to search her room, he found the imprint of an extra body in the mattress.

'Later, I had a similar experience. I always make my bed in the morning, but once, when I returned during the day, I had the feeling that something wasn't quite right. My pillows had been thrown across my bed, not placed, but hurled as in anger. I photographed them and sent the image to Chris, the landlord. He pointed out that there was also a deep imprint in the mattress of the freshly made bed.

The haunted bedroom

'The curious thing is nothing like that has happened since my sister gave me our mother's ashes and I've had them in the room… all the same, I always check my room to see if anything's amiss, although I keep everything in its place.'

The conversation turned to the inn's renowned Spanish ghost. Known to Richard and Michala as 'Roberto', he is said to have been a wealthy merchant who stayed at the Plough in 1555. He was on his way to take ship from Bristol after successful trading in the West Country and was reputedly murdered in what is now Richard's bedroom after a convivial evening's drinking with local customers.

'His attire was very smart and his drinking companions thought he had gold on his person,' said Michala. 'Once he'd staggered off to bed, they waited for him to fall asleep, sneaked upstairs and strangled him… but they never found his gold.'

'That's who we think it was who left the imprints on the mattress and causes glasses to shoot off the bar and a certain table in the lounge,' said Richard. 'You just know he's about.'

'There's nothing unpleasant, but curious things happen,' added Michala. 'For instance, Sue Davies, our cleaner, has a regular routine for cleaning the toilets. One day, she couldn't find her mop and asked me where it was… we found it lying on the carpet in front of the fireplace, where we are now and where there was no reason for it to be.'

Portsmouth Arms

'Andy – the old landlord – told us the Portsmouth Arms is haunted and he didn't like what was here,' said landlord Steve Anscombe. 'But when we took over two years ago, we felt the building heaved a sigh of relief. We loved it from the start.

'Not long after, one of our customers introduced herself as a medium. I told her the old landlord didn't like the spirits that haunted the pub. She assured me that there was nothing nasty now, that if there had been anything bad it had left with him.

'We know of two people who've died here suddenly. One was a lady, who suffered a fatal heart attack in 1867. The other was a man, who died in what's now the cellar. Again, it was heart failure, but we don't think the spirits we have here are theirs. Everything we see and hear at the pub is all right. We just talk to them…'

'But we do get a little bit scared,' interposed landlady Karen.

'True,' conceded Steve, 'we do get spooked. Sometimes my hair starts to stir and I know something's afoot. A few nights ago, I was working outside when I heard this terrific bang from upstairs. It was dead quiet, there was no wind and there was no-one here but

The bar at the Portsmouth Arms

us two, so I rushed into the bar only to find Karen sitting there, looking bemused.

'"Did you hear that?" I asked and you nodded.'

'So, I told him to go and have a look,' interjected Karen, 'and he said, "No, I'm not!"

'"Well, I'm not going up there!"' I said. Steve did go after that… but what did he pick up to defend himself? A feather duster!

'"What are you going to do with that?" I asked. "Tickle them?" Off he went upstairs… but there was nothing there.

'One afternoon before opening time, we heard three loud, heavy knocks on the front door,' continued Karen. 'We wondered who could be calling on us, but again when we went to see who had knocked, there was nobody there.

'The last time I'd heard three heavy knocks like that was the day before my cousin died. There's an old superstition that three knocks means a death is imminent. You can't disbelieve what you hear, see or touch. I said, "Something's going to happen. We'll hear of a death." This time, I heard directly afterwards that my granddaughter had lost her baby.'

The Portsmouth Arms, little changed since the photograph on page 27 was taken

As well as knocks and bangs, Steve and Karen have experienced other inexplicable sounds at the Portsmouth Arms.

'I know you get creaking floorboards in old houses like this,' said Steve, 'but we often hear footsteps on the upstairs corridor, even when we're alone. I know Karen's footsteps, but those I hear are not hers… Then there are the voices. I was in the bar one day when I heard a lady's voice right in my ear call my name. So I went into the kitchen and said, "Yes, darling, what is it?" And you said, "I didn't call you."

'I didn't think anything more of it and walked back to the bar, when I heard the voice again call my name quite forcefully. So, I went straight back to the kitchen, but again you'd said nothing to me. You had the same experience a few days later and you thought it was me calling you when I hadn't.

'Twice I saw a lady,' continued Steve. 'She was about my height, with long blonde hair. She was standing near the darts board, wearing a white, whalebone corset and skirt as they wore hundreds of years ago. I thought, "If I look directly at her, she'll move." She did: I turned about and there she was right across the room by the front door, a distance not less than twenty feet from where she had just been.'

What's it like, we asked, living in an old building with so much supernatural activity?

'I don't find these manifestations disturbing,' said Karen, and Steve nodded his agreement. 'I used to be a medium myself, part of a circle. I know there's both good and bad, but the important thing is what you attract.'

Smugglers Inn, Blue Anchor

'Although I don't like the idea of the paranormal, I'm less sceptical than I was when we first came here two years ago,' said Mark Forman, landlord of the Smugglers Inn at Blue Anchor, which is thought to originate from the 17th century.

'I don't think I'll ever truly believe until I see something with another person. I'll always try to find a reason behind things. When I was in the Army, we were put through severe sleep deprivation on

The Smugglers Inn

exercises. You see trees get up and walk away and you know it's not happening because you've only had four hours' sleep that week… but there are things here at the Smugglers that I can't explain.

'When we took over the inn in 2019 we heard two rumours of its being haunted. I know the last owner did make up a few stories just to prompt a bit of PR, but one rumour was there was an old chap in the bar and a child in what we call the naughty corner – one of the alcoves at the back of the pub.'

Mark described how one of his guests, having heard of the inn's haunted reputation, brought an electromagnetic field meter (EMF) and a camera when she stayed overnight at the Smugglers: 'She was dead excited. During the night her EMF was turned off by unseen hands before her eyes. She took a load of photos. In one of them is a very visible shadow sitting on the sofa. You can't make out its shape.'

Another couple who visited the Smugglers and showed great interest in its haunted reputation told Mark they make videos of haunted places. They promised to return with their equipment,

The 'naughty corner' at the Smugglers Inn

The bedroom where voices are heard

including voice detectors, an EMF and cameras. Ghost hunter John and his two colleagues started filming in the bar late one evening, having set up their voice detector, which emits continuous white noise. It soon picked up random voices, both in the bar, in the naughty corner and in the letting rooms upstairs. The voices identified themselves by name through the device, but there was also a voice that seemed to come from the surrounding air.

Later, John returned with the voice detector to show it to regular customers at the inn. Again, it picked up mysterious voices... and a loud voice from the surrounding atmosphere which told them to 'f*** off' in no uncertain terms. John reprimanded it, but remarked he's had similar experiences before.

'There's a lovely lady from Watchet who claims to be a medium and to talk with spirits,' continued Mark. 'After the Real Ghost Hunters video was filmed, but before it became available on Amazon Prime and U Tube, she dined here with her sister and some friends.

'I told her about how I had put out some Christmas toys in the naughty corner as the film crew had done when they made contact with a child spirit. I also told her of how I had taken photos to check whether any of the toys had been moved. They hadn't.

'Well, she absolutely tore into me: "Don't you ever, ever, ever mess with the spirits in there! They're not what you think!"

'She obviously believed what she was saying and was really vehement. Furthermore, she said there's the spirit of an angry Irishwoman in the next alcove.'

Mark went on to tell us of some of his own supernatural experiences at the Smugglers Inn: 'There have been a couple of times when my wife, Lisa, was out taking the kids to school and I was on my own when I've distinctly heard a woman's voice calling my name from upstairs, but when I went to look there was no-one there.

'Both Lisa and I have heard footsteps in Room 3, where the lady took the photograph of a shadowy form. Again, when we checked, there was nobody around.

'Last summer, my six year old boy said someone had called his

Belle at the bar

name. He thought they wanted him to play with them… yet there was nobody there. This happened again a couple of weeks later. Well, people say that if you ask spirits to leave you alone they will. I don't really believe this, but I walked around upstairs telling them to stay away from my children… just in case it does work.'

Before we left, Mark introduced us to a very large and corporeal canine presence. Belle, a Great Dane, was taking a break from whelping her new litter and greeted us with wagging tail. She was quite relaxed, but has sometimes shown signs that she has intimations of unseen presences at the Smugglers Inn

'They say that dogs are sensitive to these things,' said Mark. 'When we first got Belle she would cower at the archway leading into the bar. She also has a weird obsession with the steps leading down to the bar. She likes to sit or lie on the bottom step.'

The Staghunters, Brendon

A large inn of considerable age by the banks of the fast flowing East Lyn, the Staghunters is run by the Wyburn family. As well as guests from afield, it has a loyal following of local customers – and several supernatural presences.

'My first recollection of unexplained activity,' said Simon Wyburn, 'was in '06 when a customer said to me: "Did you know a lady has walked through your lounge wall and down to the river?" Well, I thought he'd had too many drinks, but Hayley said she'd seen the lady too and several other customers corroborated this. Years ago, it wasn't a wall but a doorway with Victorian tiles. It's like a recording from the past, when a woman working here would have taken clothes for washing in the river.'

'What I saw was like a mist, like dust motes in the shape of a lady,' added Hayley Jones, who's worked at the Staghunters for eleven years: 'She was young, with long hair and a long dress,

The Staghunters from its garden

Portrait of Johnny Coward

but I wouldn't like to commit to a full description, in case it's my imagination adding this to that. The next week, a guest reported the same thing, as did a delivery man, who saw the apparition make its way to the river.'

Several people have had supernatural experiences in the bar too, as Simon related: 'John Palfrey, who was landlord here some years before us, went to empty the till one night and found an apparition of a monk standing behind him. He was very, very frightened and ran upstairs telling his wife he'd leave the money where it was. Later, he asked a priest to come and exorcise that part of the bar.

'I've had experiences in the bar too. One evening, I was locking up with a chap called Joseph who works here, when our eyes were drawn to a light in the corridor behind. "Did you see that, Joe?" I asked. He nodded and we both went to investigate. It was a very distinct ball of light, bigger than a tennis ball and smaller that a football, travelling along the corridor at a walking pace.

'I look for a logical explanation for things, but I can't find anything to explain this orb of light, nor an incident that related to Johnny Coward.

'Johnny was a little man, a jockey and stable hand over at Oare,' continued Simon. 'You can see his portrait in the bar. He used to ride over here and his pony, well knowing the way, would take him home after he'd had a few pints and a snooze on the settle. Johnny passed away years ago but recently, when I was talking about him to his cousin, Sid, a pint glass flew off the shelf onto the floor without breaking. It was like Johnny was making his presence known.

'The locals always talk about Mary,' continued Simon. 'If something strange happens or there are unexplained footsteps "Mary did it." One day a gentleman walked in and forgot to shut the front door behind him. "Shall I shut it?" he asked. "Don't worry," I said mischievously, "Mary'll do it." Within five seconds of my saying this, the handle went up and the door closed. Now, that's a heavy door, it doesn't just open and close by itself.'

'I was behind the bar when someone tapped me on the shoulder,' added Richard, Simon's father. 'When I turned around, nobody was there. Another time, I was walking along the corridor when I had the impression someone was behind me and then I felt something go right through me – *whoosh*. That was really weird.'

Hayley has also had a strange encounter in the bar: 'Once, I thought there was a man waiting to be served, but when I looked again, he wasn't there, which made me feel a bit on edge, and I haven't felt like that for a long time.'

Another part of the Staghunters where mysterious presences make themselves felt is the chapel: 'When we first came here,' said Wendy, Simon's mother, 'I used to sit in the chapel at night after a stressful day and it was the most incredibly peaceful place, wonderful – it's my favourite part of the building. Later, we had a medium visit here who confirmed the chapel is absolutely buzzing with presences, but all the vibes are good.'

The chapel, not open to the public

Opposite: the corridor between rooms 14 and 11

'The most peculiar things happen between the 27 December and New Year,' Wendy continued. 'Doors bang and lights go on and off; things move around… there's so much energy. Once, all the glasses shot off the shelf in the bar – which is perfectly stable – and smashed on the floor.'

Various supernatural phenomena have been reported in the up-stairs bedrooms too. 'Several other customers have had feelings in Room 9,' said Simon. 'Some have taken photographs showing orbs of light. One guest who'd stayed with us before said she was happy to stay again in any bedroom but Room 9, where she had previously encountered an old lady staring at her during the night.'

Footsteps have been heard along the corridor between rooms 14 and 11 by Joy, Simon's wife, whilst Hayley refuses to stay in Room 11 because she was disturbed there by mysterious voices.

'It happened when we were snowed in at the Staghunters.

Normally, I sleep fine, but it was like the whole pub was in the room with me; people were shouting and it was like I was listening to them through headphones underwater.

'I hid under the duvet that night and changed rooms afterwards.'

More about West Country ghosts from Bossiney Books

Ghostly Encounters, Peter Underwood
Ghosts of Cornwall, Peter Underwood
Ghosts of Devon, Peter Underwood
Ghosts of Dorset, Peter Underwood
Haunted Inns of Cornwall, Robert Hesketh
Haunted Inns of Devon, Robert Hesketh
West Country Hauntings, Peter Underwood

Books about Exmoor and Devon by Robert Hesketh

Exmoor – a Shortish Guide
Really Short Walks: Exmoor and Brendon
Shortish Walks on Exmoor
The Somerset Coast: Beaches and Walks
Tearoom and Pub Walks on Exmoor

Fairly Easy Walks: North Devon
Shortish Walks in North Devon

The Devon Beach and Cove Guide
101 Things to See in Devon
Devon Castles
Devon Festivals
Devon's Geology
Devon's History
Devon's Railway Heritage
Devon Smugglers